AF379062

THE gods OF THIS WORLD

Exposing The Occults Of Modern Day Satan

THE gods OF THIS WORLD

Exposing The Occults Of Modern Day Satan

ballpublications
Christian Living. Inspiration. Faith in God

www.ball-publications.com
www.facebook.com/ballpublications

CONTENTS

The thief (Satan) comes to steal, kill and destroy;
I (Jesus) have come that they may have life, and
have it to the full. ~ John 10:10) NIV

INTRODUCTION

The thief (Satan) comes to steal, kill and destroy; I (Jesus)
have come that they may have life, and have it to the full.
-John 10:10 NIV

This scripture is powerful if you really think about it. Satan's job is to steal our joy, peace and soul. To kill our spirit and our physical bodies and to completely destroy our relationships with each other and most importantly God.

The occults in our society are nothing new. We have heard of most of them before, because God has revealed them all to us in His word. If we study and read God's word then we would not be surprised at Satan's work. But Satan is also the god of lies. He paints a pretty picture of light, so his old tricks are like new. The same activities that happened in the Bible are occurring today, except they have new names and are packaged with a nice, big bow.

Some of these re-discovered occults may not sit well with you. Or you may not have realized (like I have) that your favorite movie, book, video or board game, animated movie/cartoon or T.V. program are affiliated. These discoveries are not meant to scare you, but to open your mind and spirit to God's truth. But the disturbing point of all, is that Satan is out to destroy our children. He knows that children are discovering new things about the world and themselves everyday. They are constantly bored and looking for more and more stimulation. Because this generation has so much technology and are exposed to so much, nothing seems to

INTRODUCTION

phase them. Being good and doing right are like pulling teeth. And death or taking one's life are becoming commonplace. So the dark, unknown appeal of Satan's world are pulling our children away.

My goal is to expose the popular occults of Satan as we see it today. From witches, vampires, tattoos and gangster rap, to even yoga - these are a few examples of how Satan and his demons can gain access into our lives. And if you or loved ones are experiencing difficulty in your lives as a result of these occults, such as: addiction, depression, bitterness, suicidal thoughts and the like, and want to be delivered, you will receive relevant scriptures from God's word to fight them off. You can live the life that God intended for you to live. A life of happiness, joy, peace, truth and love!

What Is An Occult?

The word "occult" comes from the Latin word occultus, which means "knowledge of the hidden." The popular meaning is "knowledge of the paranormal." For most practicing occultists it is the study of a deeper spiritual reality that extends beyond pure reason and the physical sciences. Occultism is the study of occult practices such as: magic, alchemy, extra-sensory perception, astrology, spiritualism and divination.

Occultism has negative meanings for many people. Some religions view the occult as being supernatural or paranormal, not achieved by God and is the work of an opposing entity. Christians regard occultism as a contrast to Christian beliefs of separation between body and spirit. And that Satan and his demons are master minds of anything that is a direct contrast to God.

God forbids his people to affiliate themselves with anything dealing with Satan and the occult. Deuteronomy 18:9-13 says, "*When you enter the land the Lord your God is giving you, be very careful not to imitate the detestable customs of the nations living there. Let no one be found among you who sacrifices his son or daughter in the fire, who practices divination or sorcery, interprets omens, engages in witchcraft, or casts spells, or who is a medium or spiritist or who consults the dead. Anyone who does these things is detestable to the Lord, and because of these detestable practices the Lord your God will drive out those nations before you. You must be blameless before the Lord your God."*

There are 3 categories of the occult: **Divination, Magic/Paganism and Spiritism**. I will discuss in detail the occults used in our modern day society today. Again Satan is the master of light, and deceit. He uses subjects and objects in our everyday lives that we are unaware of, because our society and our children have become desensitized to this world. Beware of the little things in your life!

CHAPTER

2

Modern Day Divination

Divination is the attempt to foretell the future. It is the art of discovering knowledge by means of supernatural powers. These arts include: astrology, zodiac signs, crystal balls, tarot cards, palm reading, psychics, numerology, horoscopes, telepathy, charm bracelets, fortune telling, handwriting analysis, tea leaf reading and soothsayers.

ALL THINGS ASTROLOGY

These people attempt to use these items by studying the stars, planets, sun and moon. They study these things to try to predict your life or the events of this world. All of these acts of fortune telling are only used to control your mind and keep you in fear. As soon as your life goes awry you may continue to seek out one of these fortune tellers to make you feel better or tune into late night T.V. to contact a psychic. But the name "fortune" teller seems appropriate, because over the course of time, their main focus is ultimately to steal your money (or fortune). Remember Satan has come to steal.

You may have become that person who reads your own horoscope online or in a newspaper. Some of you may receive your "daily horoscope" delivered to you through *Facebook* or another form of media. Some of you can't function until you read it. However you receive it, you still are relying on your horoscope to tell you what kind of day you will have, how much money you will make or who you should become attracted to, based on his or her zodiac sign. We have all done it. I must admit that I still read my fortune cookie, with my lucky numbers - after eating at a chinese restaurant.

CHARM BRACELETS

The rediscovered and popular item of jewelry is the charm bracelet. This bracelet is usually made of stars, moons, planets, stones and the like. It has been around from some time. It may be your childs favorite piece of jewelry and made together as a favorite past time. The history of charms goes back as far as the Neolithic era. Our ancient ancestors would pick up an unusual stone or piece of wood and carry it with him to ward off his enemies. Thousands of years later, elaborate jewelry made of precious stones and metals emerged during the age of the Egyptian Pharaohs, which was when the first recognizable charm bracelets and necklaces first appeared.

Ancient Egyptians lived very short lives by today's standard - between 30 to 40 years on average. And because they had so little time on earth, they obsessively prepared for a prosperous life after death. Charm bracelets played a significant role in the preparation process. Charm wrist and neck bracelets were not only coveted as protective shields and signs of status in this life, they were also worn to help the gods guide the wearer and his or her possessions to the proper status level in the afterlife. The Egyptians worshipped pagan idol gods, so they relied on these bracelets to protect them against evil - or so they thought. Satan wants you to believe that this bracelet is simply a piece of jewelry. But this simple piece of jewelry can allow Satan to work in you or your childs life, because of its original intent.

Some Christians may think reading your own horoscope, casually visiting a fortune teller or wearing a charm bracelet is harmless, but that's exactly what Satan wants you to think. *"It's harmless. It's fun. What do you have to lose?" Right*? Well, God says in Isaiah 47:11-14, *"Disaster will come upon you, and you will not know how to conjure it away. A calamity will fall upon you that you cannot ward off with a ransom; a catastrophe you cannot foresee will suddenly come upon you. Keep on, then, with your magic spells and with your many sorceries, which you have labored at since childhood. Perhaps you will succeed, perhaps you will cause terror. All the counsel you have received has only worn you out! Let your astrologers come forward, those stargazers who make predictions month by month, let them save you from what is coming upon you. Surely they are like stubble; the fire will burn them up. They cannot even save themselves from the power of the flame. Here are no coals to warm anyone; here is no fire to sit by."* These forms of divination are not of God and those who practice them will suffer and be punished greatly by God.

Divination will only lead you into destruction. It will ultimately kill you. Divination cannot save you, only God through Jesus Christ, can do that. God has all the knowledge and wisdom you will ever need. He created the stars, moon, sun and planets as beautiful objects in our universe, but he didn't ask us to worship them. God is ultimately in control. And by believing in Him, your future life will become a reality.

CHAPTER
3

Modern Day Magic or Paganism

Magic or paganism is the attempt to control you or the environment by performing a ceremony, charm or casting spells. These arts include: witchcraft, sorcery, black or white magic, voodoo, charmers, enchanters, wizards, witch doctors, vampires and tattoos on the body.

SORCERY

These people can use objects to bring harm to you and your family. The charmer can cast spells and create magical healings. He can also call demons and evil spirits to perform his acts of deceit. The enchanter is a hisser or whisperer of magic spells. And a sorcerer or magician can manipulate supernatural powers to control others through evil spirits. He will try to hurt you by also casting spells, curses and working with the wicked. The witch also whispers spells and performs magic. And the practice of witchcraft is a form of religion that manipulates nature and supernatural forces by using fertility rituals. Witches (female) or Wizards (male) may use clairvoyance, divination, magic and casting spells to control your life. And they are required to participate in a pagan ceremony called Great Rite. This ceremony may include sex and other occult activities.

Black magic, which is evil, is an attempt to bring harm to you resulting in misfortune or death. And white magic, which is good, is an attempt to undo harm and use forces for good. But let's be clear, there is no such thing as a "good witch." A witch is a witch - is a witch.

People who practice witchcraft or magic is also an abomination of God. God says that he will judge and be a swift witness against them. And they deserve death in the lake of fire as well as all who practice and believe in these things. Wizards and those who follow them are defiled and he warns us not to seek after them, because they are wicked. Exodus 22:18 says, *"Do not allow a sorceress to live."* And 1 Samuel 15:23 says, *"For rebellion is like the sin of divination and arrogance like the evil of idolatry. Because you have rejected the word of the Lord, he has rejected you as King."*

HARRY POTTER

The *Harry Potter* series of books in our modern day society has become some sort of a cult of its' own. *Harry Potter*, according to Wikipedia, is a series of seven fantasy novels written by the British author J. K. Rowling. The adventures of the adolescent wizard Harry Potter and his best friends Ron Weasley and Hermione Granger are all students at Hogwarts School of Witchcraft and Wizardry. The main story is about Harry's quest to overcome the evil wizard Lord Voldemort, whose goal is to subjugate non-magical people, conquer the wizard world and destroy everyone who stands in his way - especially Harry. Today these books have now become movies and is the highest grossing film series of all time. The *Harry Potter* brand is worth in excess of $15 billion dollars.

It should not be surprising that witchcraft or wizards and warlocks are popular with our children. Satan has used this British author to do his work, by promoting a fantasy world of magic in today's society. She has even publicly acknowledged researching Wicca for her books. Satan has captured our children's, and even adults, attention by promoting meditation, sorcery and transfiguration into other beings or animals, which can lead to Satanism. The *Harry Potter* series can introduce your children to human and animal sacrifice. And the Wicca religion can use this tool to have your children accept witchcraft as normal.

It's really disturbing how today's society and even Christians have been convinced that it's just a fictional story - a fantasy world. But that's just what Satan wants you to believe, because it gives him another way to enter into you or your childs life and try to destroy it. Because *Harry Potter* toys and games are now sold to our children to imitate magic and magic spells, this gives Satan and his demons another way to enter and plant themselves into our loved ones lives. Even wearing a *Harry Potter* Halloween costume can plant the seed of destruction.

Thousands of kids are now seeking information on the internet about schools of witchcraft that they can attend. And when J. K. Rowling was asked about new ideas of her next book, she said, *"I can tell you that the books are getting darker. Harry's going to have quite a bit to deal with as he gets older."*

We as parents need to be aware of the subtleties of Satan. All he needs is a small way to enter into your life. And he uses any and every way that he can.

BLACK MAGIC VS. WHITE MAGIC

We all remember *The Wizard Of Oz* as a classic movie. Glinda was the good witch, who was beautiful, pure and wore white. She used her magic for good and not evil. She gave Dorothy her ruby slippers and helped her find her way home. And the Wicked Witch of the West was an evil witch, who tried to stop Dorothy and her friends from seeing the Wizard. She was ugly, wore black, and tried to cause harm. In the movie, it was always good vs evil. Even though Dorothy and her friends had to go through their adventure, the good witch and the evil witch were always present. Much as in the world today, we live in a world where good vs evil is always present. But much like Dorothy going home, God has always been there for us, so we can always find our way back home to Him.

Because evil is always present, Satan never wants us to find our way back to God if we become lost. He will use "the yellow brick road" of life to get us off the path, which is of God. But in the end, just as Dorothy, if we just ask, God will always bring us back.

The word of God makes no distinction between good or evil occults, good vs evil witches or black and white magic. God condemns them all. For 2 Corinthians 11:14-15 says, *"And no wonder, for Satan himself masquerades as an angel of light. It is not surprising, then, if his servants masquerade as servants of righteousness. Their end will be what their actions deserve."* After learning about magic and what it can do to you and your family, the next step should be to rid your home of anything affiliated. Even the people of Ephesus knew that witchcraft was wrong because they publicly burned their books dealing with this occult. (Acts 19:19)

Satan and his demon's powers are no match to God's power. Even when Pharoah used his magicians to throw down the staffs of Satan, to turn into serpants, Aaron and Moses one staff of God, also turned into a serpant and swallowed up the staffs of Satan, defeating him. (Exodus 7:10-12) Enough said.

VOODOO

Voodoo is a pagan religion with Western Indian and West Africa elements. This word, from the West Africa term, means "spirit." It was brought by West African slaves to Haiti, where it is now the dominant religion. It first entered the U.S. after the Haitian revolt of 1804.

Voodoo is used as a form of sorcery rituals and a trance like state to communicate with ones who have died, saints and animals-like idols. People who practice voodoo can use charms, spells, curses and the like. They also practice voodoo by placing objects such as, pins and needles into another object-like doll to adversely affect them in a negative way. They believe that casting a spell on this object will cause harm to the person or object involved.

There are two main types of voodoo: *Petro* which is dominated by black magic and *Rada* which is seen as benign. Voodoo believers worship a god called *Bondeye*. And humans deal with three types of spirits called: *Lemiste*, *Lemo* and *Lemarasa*. After death, they believe one part of man's spirit goes to this god *Bondeye* and another goes to *Gine*, which is an African spiritual homeland. Believers also believe in reincarnation, which means that after one dies they come back to earth to live in a new life form.

People who practice voodoo also use sorcery and black magic in their rituals. They may beat on drums, speak through other worshippers and include animal sacrifices to worship the spirits. In the U.S., voodoo is most common in New Orleans, Chicago, New York and Miami, where areas of Haitian immigrants are prevalent. It is even believed that voodoo brings a curse of disobedience upon the land, which we saw in the disasters in New Orleans and Haiti. (Deuteronomy 28:15-19).

Voodoo is not something discussed everyday. It is always a taboo and dark subject to discuss. And because of this, a lot of people are left ignorant to this occult. But again God calls voodoo a lie. Jeremiah 27:9-10 says, *"So do not listen to your prophets, your diviners, your interpreters of dreams, your mediums or your sorcerers who tell you. 'You will not serve the King of Babylon.' They prophesy lies to you that will only serve to remove you far from your lands; I will banish you and you will perish."* The opposing purpose of voodoo is to destroy, bring poverty, darkness, loss, storms and natural disasters to your life. But the ultimate purpose is to turn you away from God and His righteousness.

VAMPIRES

What is a vampire? The vampire is a mythological being who is said to exist by drinking blood of other people, usually by biting their necks, after which the victim also becomes a vampire who seeks new victims. The vampire legend can be traced back to medieval and Eastern European folklore. But variations of tales of vampire-like creatures also exist in Africa, Asia and America.

The popularity of the teen romance novels in the *Twilight* series has given rise to a renewed interest in vampires. *Twilight* is a series of four vampire-themed fantasy romance novels named *Twilight, New Moon, Eclipse* and *Breaking*

Dawn, all written by Stephenie Meyer. It charts a period in the life of Isabella "Bella" Swan, a teenage girl who moves to Forks, Washington, and falls in love with a 104 year old vampire named Edward Cullen, who drinks animal blood rather than human blood. The books are based on the vampire myth, but *Twilight* vampires differ in a number of particulars from the general vampire lore. For instance, *Twilight* vampires have strong piercing teeth rather than fangs; they glitter in sunlight rather than burn; and they can drink animal blood as well as human blood. Meyer, who is a Mormon, acknowledges that her faith has influenced her work. In particular, she says that her characters *"tend to think more about where they came from, and where they are going, than might be typical."*

The Vampire Diaries series premiered on the CW Network on September 10, 2009 and is currently in its third season. It is an American teen supernatural drama based on the book series of the same name. The series takes place in Mystic Falls, Virginia, a fictional small town haunted by supernatural beings. The main focus of the series is the love triangle between Elena Gilbert and Stefan and Damon, all of whom have dark pasts. The original pilot episode attracted the largest audience of any series premiere since the network began in 2006.

While fantasy fiction such as *Twilight* and *The Vampire Diaries* are probably for the most part harmless, any obsessive interest in vampires or the occult are unhealthy. It is a dangerous time for some, since many of the seemingly "harmless" involvements associated with Halloween can also become entries for the occult. Halloween can become a "crossover" in which innocent games can lead to serious entanglement with real witches, neo-pagans, new agers and real practicing vampires, who have a website that shows ways to get human and animal blood safely and legally. A weak, emotionally fragile young teen, whose life is stressed, or has low self-esteem issues or lack of a strong role model, can be persuaded very easily to join or believe in these occults. These interests are open doors for Satan and his demons to take over their mind and spirit. For 1 Peter 5:8 says, *"Be sober-minded; be watchful. Your adversary the devil prowls around like a roaring lion, seeking someone to devour."*

We are also reminded in Philippians 4:8 to *"fill our minds with "whatever is lovely, whatever is admirable - if anything is excellent or praiseworthy."* Instead of young teen girls looking to a fictional, perfected character in "Edward" of the *Twilight* series, they should look to Christ for perfection. Once they seek God first, then they will see true character in the young man God brings to them in a future husband. Instead of young teen boys looking to "Bella" for a fictional and alluring beauty, they should seek Christ and allow Him to find true inner beauty in his future wife.

There are two things that vampires fear most - the light and the cross. Jesus Christ is the light of the world and the cross was to set the captives (vampires) free. For John 8:12 says, *"When Jesus spoke again to the people, he said, "I am the light of the world. Whoever follows me will never walk in darkness, but have the light of life."* Vampires deal with lifestyle principles that go against God's word. They function only in darkness. They became bats or were bitten by bats that began the vampire infection. Vampires and their movies promote fear. Horror comes as a result of wickedness. And lastly, vampires promote death and not life.

Christian families should avoid vampires and all things related to the occult world. Parents who find their teens going through this debate or phase should read God's word to them. And by doing so, they will see that occults contradict God's word. Ultimately, the decision to read or view these materials is the responsibility of the parents, because the parent is held accountable for leading and guiding their children in God's ways. We have been trained to beware of witches, magic, astrology, tarot cards and the like, but the newest enemy to beware of is the vampire. Because he is a seductively attractive, charismatic figure who has a great deal of appeal to our teens.

TATTOOS

Tattoos on ones body is as common today as it was in the bible days. Tattoos are done to mark the body with symbols and art that depict ones life or decorate ones skin. Whatever you may go through emotionally, can end up as a reflection on your body. Heavy Metal Rock, Hip Hop, Gangsta Rap and athletic stars, have caused tattoos to hit mainstream and commonplace. And because our children idolize these stars, they want to copy everything they do. Unfortunately, tattoos are nothing new and it was practiced as a pagan ritual to appease the gods.

How did tattoos start? Babylonian and Canaanite prostitutes would tattoo themselves as part of their worship. Baal worshippers, who was an idol god, wore tattoos on their hands to receive more power. This is the reason for the major increase of tatto use. These nations were against God and His practices, so they embraced pagan practices to worship Satan. Satan is pushing his occult religions back to Earth, so he can be worshipped. 1 Corinthians 10:19-21 says, *"Do I mean then that a sacrifice offered to an idol is anything, or that an idol is anything? No, but the sacrifices of pagans are offered to demons, not to God, and I do not want you to be participants with demons. You cannot drink the cup of the Lord and the cup of demons too; you cannot have a part in both the Lord's table and the table of demons."* Because tattoos are considered to be a part of idol worship, God says you can't serve two masters. You have to choose.

Another form of tattooing prevalent in the African or African American cultures are scarification. Scarification is cutting into the skin with a sharp instrument, then rubbing it with ashes or plants to form a permanent blister on the skin. Charcoal or gun powder is then rubbed into the blister to make it stand out. This practice is used a lot in African American fraternities or in the prison communities. Leviticus 19:28 says, *"Do not cut your bodies for the dead or put tattoo marks on yourselves. I am the Lord."* This scripture clearly says that God does not approve of <u>any</u> tattoos and never did. And because God is against it, Satan glorifies and abuses it. The root of tattooing never changes. It will always be a pagan, spiritual ritual.

The ultimate purpose of tattoos is to desensitize ourselves to cutting and marking our bodies. Satan's goal is to prepare our generation and the generations to come for the coming of the Antichrist (Satan in human form). When the Antichrist comes he will require the number 666 to be tattooed on their foreheads and hands. So if you can easily get a tattoo today, when the 666 number becomes a requirement, you will already be accustomed to the system of body marking. It's all a part of Satan's plan. For Revelation 13:16-18 says, *"He also forced everyone, small and great, rich and poor, free and slave, to receive a mark on his right hand or on his forehead, so that no one could buy or sell unless he had the mark, which is the name of the beast or the number of his name. This calls for wisdom. If anyone has insight, let him calculate the number of the beast, for it is man's number - His number is 666."*

If you are a Christian who struggles with this issue, just know that God does not approve. You may feel that Christian or non-evil tattoos are acceptable. But God says <u>all</u> markings on your body, which is the temple of God, are unacceptable. If you have already put a tattoo on your body, out of ignorance, you can still repent and ask God for forgiveness. God doesn't want us to continue in sin. Once we know what God disapproves of, we are held accountable to Him. Many tattoo images today contain symbols such as: serpents, skulls and crossbones, which promote death. And sexual tattoos can also invite the spirit of lust and perversion into your life. Please pray to God to help you with this issue. And by doing this, the Holy Spirit and God's word won't steer you wrong.

Modern Day Spiritism

People who practice spiritism attempt to communicate with the spirits of the dead. They seek them out to try and receive information from them, by performing seances, meditations, necromancy, or using Ouija boards and ghost-like spirits. Mediums, Psychics and Spiritists believe that they can communicate with the dead or that the dead come to them to relay messages to loved ones left on earth. Some try to use this for good, by helping law enforcement solve missing person or murder cases.

SEANCES

Seance rituals call forth: spirits, ghosts, guardians, guides and demons by performing a ceremony to open pathways to the spirits to contact those who have passed away. They can use meditation, Ouija boards, pendulums and even tarot cards as methods of communication. Meditation combined with candles and incense can also be used. Seances date back 4500 years ago in Egypt, during the reign of Pharaoh

Khufu, known as Cheops. He was most likely the builder of the Great Pyramid at Giza.

Modern day groups today who believe in the paranormal such as: Wicca or witchcraft groups evolve around seance rituals. Indian Shamanism and Christians who call on the "Holy Spirit" to speak in tongues are considered to be a part of this group. But let's make things clear that God, who is also the true "Holy Spirit," is no way a part of this occult. In Native American culture, the Shaman acted as an intermediary between the physical and spirit worlds. Also known as a medicine man, the Shaman was an important position in Indian culture. But in the book of Acts there are three occasions were speaking in tongues accompanied the receiving of the Holy Spirit. Acts 2:4, 10:44-46 and 19:6 are the only places in the Bible where speaking in tongues is an evidence of receiving the Holy Spirit. Even though believers who accept Jesus as their Lord and Savior has received the Holy Spirit, not every believer speaks in tongues. God has given all believers different gifts to be used for His glory. For 1 Corinthians 12:29-31 says, *"Are all apostles? Are all prophets? Are all teachers? Do all work miracles? Do all have gifts of healing? Do all speak in tongues? Do all interpret? But eagerly desire the greater gifts."* Speaking in tongues is a miraculous gift that has a specific purpose. But God is the God of light, he can't dwell in darkness, which is what this occult is.

PSYCHICS & MEDIUMS

Psychics or mediums claim the ability to contact spirits of the dead, angels, demons or other entities. A medium, defined by the Oxford English Dictionary, is *"a person believed to be in contact with the spirits of the dead who communicate between the living and the dead."* They claim to listen to, relay messages from, and relate conversations with spirits. They may go into a trance-like state to allow a spirit to control their body and speak through it.

Mental mediums communicate with spirits by telepathy. The medium can hear, see or feel messages from spirits. When a medium does a "reading" for a person, that person then becomes the "sitter."

Physical mediums is a manipulation of energies by spirits. It may involve loud raps, noises, voices, objects or body parts such as: hands and levitation. The medium is used as a source of power for such spirits. And direct voice communication uses the medium's voice as a way to communicate with the living during seances.

Psychic and mediums have now become so popular, that the media has created multiple T.V. shows and movies about them. From *Psychic Detectives, Psychic Witness, Psychic Investigators, Medium, Ghost Whisperer, Haunting Evidence, The 4400, The Dead Zone, Paranormal Activity and Millennium,* just to name a few. Famous psychic mediums include: John Edward, Sylvia Browne, Allison Dubois, George Anderson and James Van Praagh. These movies, T.V. shows and famous psychics, allow these occult forces to enter into your homes, which creates disaster.

Again, Satan uses all that he can to make light of this occult. People are becoming more and more faithless and vunerable to the spirit world. Instead of relying on God and His wisdom, we are relying on people. God says that those who seek information from familiar spirits are defiled and deserve death. 1 Chronicles 10:13-14 says, *"Saul died because he was unfaithful to the Lord; he did not keep the word of the Lord and even consulted a medium for guidance, and did not inquire of the Lord. So the Lord put him to death and turned the kingdom over to David son of Jesse."*

God also calls the necromancer or those who call

upon the dead, an abomination. This person communicates with a demonic spirit, which is familiar with the dead person. The necromancer then believes that he has the ability to contact the spirit of that dead person, which is actually the demon posing as the dead person. Examples of current T.V. shows are the *Ghost Whisperer* with Jennifer Love Hewitt and *Crossing Over* with John Edwards.

YOGA

The word "yoga" means "union," and the goal is to unite one's transitory or temporary self with the infinite Brahman, which is the Hindu concept of God. This god is not a being, but is a spiritual entity that is one with nature and the cosmos. Pantheism is the belief that everything is God, consisting only of the universe and nature. The yoga philosophy makes no distinction between man and God. The practice of yoga is based on the belief that man and God are one.

Yoga is an ancient practice from India. It is believed to be the path to spiritual growth and enlightenment. Hatha yoga focuses on the physical body through special postures, breathing, exercises and meditation. In 150 A.D. the yoga Patamjali put yoga into eight "limbs" in his yoga sutras. The limbs are like a staircase leading you from ignorance to enlightenment. The eight limbs are: Yama (self control), Niyama (religions observance), Asana (posture), Pranayama (breathing exercises), Pratyahara (sense control), Dharana (concentration), Dhyana (deep contemplation) and Samadhi (enlightenment). All false religions seem to offer some higher knowledge that promises peace, success, happiness and tranquility in life.

It is dangerous for Christians to think that yoga is innocent. Because yoga has come back more now than ever, we have been led to believe that it's just another physical exercise to strengthen, heal, prevent bodily ailments and improve flexibility. However, the philosophy of yoga reveals it is more than a health program. It is a path to spiritual growth through Hindu gods. Yoga originated with a blatantly anti-Christian philosophy and that philosophy has not changed since its origination. It teaches a person to focus on yourself instead of the true God. And encourages people to seek answers to difficult questions of life within themselves instead of in the Word of God. It is little more than self-worship that's wrapped up in a beautiful present disguised as spirituality.

When I started noticing yoga coming back into mainstream, I was like most of you. I thought it was another exercise to help strengthen the body and lose weight. It was all over T.V. and offered in the gyms as another popular exercise. But the more I saw yoga and how it seemed to explode, I started feeling like something was wrong. When I noticed how people were "meditating" and moving their bodies, it looked like a spiritual worship, rather than just another exercise. And I started thinking that if I felt this way, others probably felt this way too. I was going with the flow to believe yoga was just another great exercise - nothing spiritual.

But again, Satan is a deceiver. He continues to use anything he can to turn us away from God, in order to worship worthless, idol gods. For 2 Kings 17:15 says, *"They rejected his decrees and the covenant he had made with their fathers and the warnings he had given them. They followed worthless idols and themselves became worthless. They imitated the nations around them although the Lord had ordered them. "Do not do as they do," and they did the things the Lord had forbidden them to do."*

If you are looking for a exercise program to take care of your body, there are numerous healthy options that are available to you. But it is not wise for a Christian to be involved in yoga. Because as stated before, it incorporates devil worship. Anything against God is the form of Satan. And we are always to keep our thoughts and behaviors on things of God and not of this world.

Why the occult is so popular

The occult is so popular because God has allowed Satan to rule this world at the present time. God has given Satan an amount of time to try and capture as many souls as he can. Because God allows us to choose between him and Satan, he has given Satan a chance to lie, deceive and tempt us away from God. Satan wants us to believe in other things instead of God. He created idols, demons and occult beliefs to take our minds off of God and onto him. Satan also want us to believe that we are gods and we are in complete control over our own lives, such as in the yoga occult. For Isaiah 47:10 says, *"You have trusted in your wickedness and have said, 'No one sees me." "Your wisdom and knowledge mislead you when you say to yourself, 'I am, and there is none besides me."*

The occult gives people a chance to believe in something else besides Christianity. They can't understand the absolute belief in good vs. evil. They want to believe in a gray area, so they won't feel guilty when mistakes are made. They also want to believe that hypocrites are in the church and people worship man (pastor, bishop or pope) more than God. But the mistake in this belief is that God is a God of second, third, fourth, etc. chances. God is the church. And He welcomes all to come. He knows you will make mistakes because you are human. He also knows how great Satan is in deceiving you into believing his truth. But he doesn't want you to be deceived, he wants you all to live. The lie Satan wants you to believe is that good vs. evil doesn't exist. He wants you to believe in what you see and hear and not have faith in a higher power - or God. The Bible says in Ephesians 6:12 *"For our struggle is not against flesh and blood, but against the rulers, against the authorities, against the spiritual forces of evil in the heavenly realms."* This scripture clearly tells us in God's word that our souls are at play. The war between good vs. evil is to compete for our souls in the end. God gave us the will to choose who we would serve. And when the Lord comes back again, Satan and his followers will be condemned to hell.

People who believe in occults feel a sense of belonging. They may be missing something from their families. They may feel unloved or uncared for. They feel that they just don't fit in anywhere. Satan wants you to feel alone. That no one cares. He wants you to feel unloved and uncared for, so he can plant these lies into your head. He may have caused the turmoil in your family to occur. Or he may have created constant pain in your life. You might not get along with family or friends. And you may feel abandoned by your church. Then an occult comes along that makes you feel that it has all the answers. It finally gets you!

But Satan wants to isolate you from your loved ones and the church, so he can work on your mind and trap you. He is the creator of confusion and depression. He wants to control your mind, so you will do his will and not God's. But God is a God of love. If no one else loves you - God does. He loves you so much that he allowed his only son's death, so we may live eternally with him. For 1 John 4:9-10 says, *"This is how God showed his love among us: He sent his one and only son into the world that we might live through him. This is love: not that we loved God, but that he loved us and sent his son as an atoning sacrifice for our sins."* You are never alone in this world, because you can now belong to God.

People are always curious about things they cannot see. They want to create their own gods according to their own religion. The concept of believing in an invisible God is a far-fetched one for some people. If they can't see it, feel it or touch it, it must not exist. So instead of believing in the one true God, whom you can't see, their minds create gods that they can see or relate to.

Idol gods were created in the bible on a constant basis. They didn't want to worship a God that they couldn't see. And because of this, Satan caused people to doubt God, which led to idol gods that they could see or believe in. The worship of Baal was a popular false god, that the Canaanites believed in. Baal can refer to any god and even to humans as a substitute for Hadad, which was a god of the rain, thunder, fertility and agriculture and the lord of Heaven. (Deuteronomy 4:2-4)

Now in our modern day, people are still worshipping gods that are man-made. From Buddha, nature, saints in the church and even man, we still feel more comfortable praying to, bowing down and worshipping things or people that we can see. But God, who is a spirit, says that idol worshipping is forbidden. Exodus 20:4 says, *"You shall not make for yourself an idol in the form of anything in heaven above or on the earth beneath or in the waters below."* Idols made by man are only images. They can't breath, talk or hear. Only the true God can do that. God says in Psalm 135:15-18 that *"the idols of the nations are silver and gold, made by the hands of men. They have mouths, but cannot speak, eyes, but they cannot see; they have ears, but cannot hear, or is there breath in their mouths. Those who make them will be like them, and so will all who trust in them."* Even though you cannot see God, he's always there.

God doesn't always have to approach you in the fire or the storm. He can come as a whisper in your ear, a smile on your face or just love in your heart.

People have a desire to control you. People who don't have control over their own lives, feel a need to control others. They may be angry at the world because their life is not going according to their plan. So they take it out on family and friends instead of looking deep inside at the bigger picture. They are unhappy because they have a void in their lives. So when you are successful and happy, they envy you because they want you to feel sad like they do. They become jealous. They despise you. They may even grow to hate you. Satan has now found a way to enter.

He uses these feelings to control us. You may be trying to control others, but Satan is actually controlling you to be his puppet. He uses these feelings of jealousy, envy and hate to destroy you and other's lives. Hate eats you up and can actually kill you physically and spiritually. It can also cause you to kill. But even if you don't physically kill someone, just hating them is the same as killing them in God's eyes. 1 John 3:15 says, *"Anyone who hates his brother is a murderer and you know that no murderer has eternal life in him."*

God also tells us we will be hated, because of Him. He was hated, abused and rebuked by men. So we as Christians, who believe in Him, will be treated the same. For John 15:18-19 says, *"If the world hates you, keep in mind that it hated me first. If you belonged to the world, it would love you as its own. As it is, you do not belong to the world, but I have chosen you out of the world. That is why the world hates you."*

The only way to destroy the feeling of control is to love God first, then your neighbor. Your neighbor includes everyone that you come into contact with - friends, family, strangers and even your enemies. It's hard to imagine loving an enemy. But God commands us to do so, even when we don't understand why. Matthew 5:43-45 says, *"You have heard that it was said, 'Love your neighbor and hate your enemy. But I tell you; Love your enemies and pray for those who persecute you, that you may be sons of your Father in heaven."* And 1 John 4:20-21 also says, *"If anyone says, "I love God," yet hates his brother, he is a liar. For anyone who does not love his brother, whom he has seen, cannot love God, whom he has not seen. And he has given us this command: Whoever loves God must also love his brother."*

Once you start doing as God commands, you won't have the desire to control others. You can't do it by yourself. The void in your heart can only be replaced by God's love.

CHAPTER
6

Some Occults in the media that you may or may not be aware of

<u>Books</u>

A Course In Miracles
A New Earth
Eat, Pray, Love
Harry Potter Series
Lord Of The Flies
Lord Of The Rings
The Hobbit
The Secret
The Shack
Twilight Series
Women, Food and God

T.V. Programs

Buffy The Vampire Slayer
Ghost Whisperer
Heroes
Lost
Medium
Moonlight
New Amsterdam
Pushing Daisies
Reaper
Six Feet Under
Supernatural
True Blood
Once Upon A Time

Movies

Avatar
Blair Witch Project
Fright Night
Ghost
Harry Potter
Nightmare On Elm St.
Paranormal Activity
Percy Jackson
Sixth Sense

The Craft
The Devil's Advocate
Twilight Saga

Animated Movies/T.V. Cartoons

Aladdin
Alice in Wonderland
American Dragon: Jake Long
Dragon Ball Z
Dragon Tales
Family Guy
Hercules
Little Mermaid
South Park
The Princess And The Frog
Yu-Gi-Oh
Cinderella

Video Games

Afro Samurai
Call of Cthulu: Dark Corners Of The Earth
Dragon Age
Final Fantasy
God Of War Series

Grand Theft Auto Series
Mortal Combat
World Of Warcraft
Resident Evil Series
The Darkness

Toys & Games

Bloody Mary
Dungeons & Dragons
Light As A Feather, Stiff As A Board
Ouija Board
Magic 8 Ball
Paper Fortune Teller
Pokemon
Spoon Bending
Voodoo Doll

CHAPTER
7

How the occult can affect you & your home

"Neither shalt thou bring an abomination into thine house, lest thou be a cursed thing like it: but thou shalt utterly detest it, and thou shalt utterly abhor it; for it is a cursed thing. (Deuteronomy 7:25-26)

God says that idols or things associated with the occult are not to be brought into our homes. These things can bring and leave curses and destroy our homes. Objects that represent idol gods give demons permission to bring their evil along with them. And once they get permission, they can't wait to try and destroy you and your children.

Here are some affects that the occult can have. Please be aware if one or more situations have occurred or are occurring in your home.

Drugs, alcohol and sexual addictions

Having anorexia, bulimia or being overweight

Having behaviorial problems that are unacceptable

Having bitterness or unable to forgive

Becoming obsessive over something or someone

Telling lies or being deceitful

Lack of motivation, sleep or having severe depression

Becoming very emotional or unmoved by a bad experience

Not wanting to be a part of other's lives

Seeing objects moving or seeing faces and figures

Being antisocial or alone all of the time

Being violent or surges of rage and anger

Having suicidal thoughts or attempting to take one's life

Cursing God and the Bible

Having nightmares and terrors

Having hallucinations, being confused or mental illness

Hearing voices to hurt yourself or others

Having strong sense of fear or having phobias

Feeling great guilt even after asking God for forgiveness

SOME MODERN DAY ACTIVITIES WITH DEMONIC INFLUENCES

Hard/Heavy Metal Rock, Gangster Rap, Auto writing, Aliens, Hindu/Eastern philosophies, Transcendental meditation, Yoga, Mind control, Unbiblical healing, Reincarnation, Martial arts, Books/objects in the home, Occult games, Hypnotism, Tattoos

HOW TO TELL IF YOUR CHILD IS EXPOSED TO THE OCCULT

1. Having a altar/candles in bedroom, closet, basement
2. Having tattoos, scars, cuts and scratches on their body
3. Reading occult type books or magazines
4. Listening to heavy metal, gangster rap or occult music
5. T.V. programs, movies and DVD's as previously discussed
6. Withdrawing from routine activities, school and friends
7. Becoming involved with knives and/or blood, i.e. cutting
8. Wearing skulls, bones and death symbols on clothing
9. Withdrawing from life, unusual seclusion, secretive
10. Becoming obsessed with death, suicidal

Seeing one or more of these symptoms with your child does not necessarily mean that they are involved with an occult. They may be going through a hard time just being a child or teenager. As long as you stay active in your child's life, by leading, teaching and guiding them in God's ways, then they won't become easily persuaded to follow others.

Scriptures to read to your children: **John 10:10,** *"The thief comes only to steal and kill and destroy; I have come that they may have life, and have it to the full."* **Ephesians 6:10-18,** *"Finally, be strong in the Lord and in his mighty power. Put on the full armor of God so that you can take your stand against the devil's schemes. For our struggle is not against flesh and blood, but against the rulers, against the authorities, against the powers of this dark world and against the spiritual forces of evil in the heavenly realms.*

Therefore put on the full armor of God , so that when the day of evil comes, you may be able to stand your ground, and after you have done everything, to stand. Stand firm then, with the belt of truth buckled around your waist, with the breastplate of righteousness in place, and with your feet fitted with the readiness that comes from the gospel of peace. In addition to all this, take up the shield of faith, with which you can extinguish all the flaming arrows of the evil one. Take the helmet of salvation and the sword of the Spirit, which is the word of God. And pray in the Spirit on all occasions with all kinds of prayers and requests. With this in mind, be alert and always keep on praying for all the saints."
Deuteronomy 5:7-9, *"You shall have no other gods before me. You shall not make for yourself an idol in the form of anything in heaven above or on the earth beneath or in the waters below. You shall not bow down to them or worship them; for I, the Lord your God, am a jealous God, punishing the children for the sin of the fathers to the third and fourth generation of those who hate me."*

Note: These diagnosis or affects on your children or in your home are only used as general guidance purposes.

CHAPTER
8

How to be delivered from the occult

Recognize and confess that you are involved in the occult. This is the first step in being delivered from the occult world. If you don't first acknowledge that you have a problem, you can't be saved. Satan's job is to keep us ignorant of God's truth. He doesn't want us to know the right way to live, which will lead to God's blessings. 1 Thessalonians 4:13 says, *"Brothers, we do not want you to be ignorant about those who fall asleep, or to grieve like the rest of men, who have no hope."*

All of us should attempt to read God's word as often as we can, and even on a daily basis, to prepare ourselves to do the best job for the Lord. We should give the world no cause to call us ignorant. If we don't know God's word, then we won't know what he approves or disapproves of. We will do and accept anything into our lives.

Remove all objects, music, books, jewelry (charms), paraphernalia, movies, idol statutes, masks, new age, witchcraft and voodoo dolls. (Deuteronomy 7:25-26, Acts 19:19) These items need to be disposed of in your home, so you won't continue to be tempted to use them. These items can be cursed by Satan and his demons. And can continue to destroy your home.

Satan uses music to influence you and your children. The influence of gangster rap or hard rock can promote death, so eliminating this music genre from your home will help. Reading books about different occults such as, witch-craft can open doors for Satan to influence your mind into trying it out. Just simple curiosity is where it starts.

Even having African masks can allow Satan to enter your home. Ethnic art in home decor is very popular now. Some people may like an eclectic look, where their home re-flects their world travels. By using masks as decor, Satan can use these items as a form of idolatry. It may seem innocent, but that's what Satan wants you to believe.

Stop associating with mediums, spiritists, horoscope read-ers, witchcraft (white or black), games or anyone who is occult influenced. 1 Corinthians 15:33-34 says, *"Do not be misled. Bad company corrupts character. Come back to your senses as you ought, and stop sinning; for there are some who are ignorant of God - I say this to your shame."*
Continuing to associate with these people or items will encourage you to stay involved. When you continue to support them, they will continue to tell you what you want to hear. Satan knows how to manipulate you into believing it's the truth. Even when viewing popular mediums on T.V., you still can invite Satan in, because the more you become involved the more you start believing.

Remember Satan's demons trick you into believing that these people or items have power, but it's the demons power that's being used.

Accept Jesus Christ as your Lord and Savior. Once you realize you have been living in darkness and want to change your life for the better, you have to invite Jesus into your life. You can't change your life, only God can do that. Romans 10:9 says, *"That if you confess with your mouth, "Jesus is Lord," and believe in your heart that God raised him from the dead, you will be saved."* Once you get saved, you transition from the power of darkness into the power of light. For 1 Peter 2:9 says, *"But you are a chosen people, a royal priesthood, a holy nation, a people belonging to God, that you may declare the praises of him who called you out of darkness into his wonderful light."*

You must pray the blood of Jesus every day. Being in constant prayer will keep your mind and spirit clean. You must search the scriptures in God's word on a daily basis to renew your mind. The struggle of old habits can constantly keep you weak. And scriptures based on the area you struggle with will keep your mind renewed. God's word will replace your occult mind with a Godly mind. And you will seek to do God's will and not your own.

Satan will continue to try and attack you, but God will give you the power to overcome him. Because you have accepted Christ in your life, God gives you the power to defeat Satan and his demons. You, as a person, are powerless. But when God comes into your heart, you receive His power. Luke 10:19 says, *"I have given you authority to trample on snakes and scorpions and to overcome all the power of the enemy; nothing will harm you."*

You now belong to God! The demons can still tempt you, but now they have to leave your soul alone.

Seek out a church or Christian group that teaches directly from God's word in the Bible. There are many churches, or leaders in the church, that don't preach totally from God's word. They may only preach a portion to make it adapt to what people want to hear and not the total truth. They want you to feel good and preach half truths, so they can justify their lifestyles. But the church of God is held accountable for one another. You are a part of the body of Christ and Christ is the head.

If you are struggling with any issues in life, including the occult, and it's brought to the people of the church or the pastor, they have an obligation to pray, care and keep you spiritually accountable. They must preach the truth in its' entirety. 1 Corinthians 12:25 says, *"So that there should be no division in the body, but that its parts should have equal concern for each other."*

We gain our strength from others in the church. And God's word keeps us focused on what he wants for us. Some people feel that they may not need to attend church, because they have a "personal" relationship with God. But church and the body of Christ gives us strength when we are weak to forces of evil. Hebrews 10:25 says, *"Let us not give up meeting together, as some are in the habit of doing, but let us encourage one another - and all the more as you see the Day approaching."* The last place Satan wants you to be, is in church. Because he knows if you are in the constant midst of fellow believers, his power is eliminated.

Always keep striving to grow in your new or renewed walk with God. Make the word of God a major part in your life. And with daily prayer and devotional time with God, your old occult life will be a thing of the past. Be blessed.

Made in the USA
Monee, IL
07 July 2026

56551139R00036